Jungle Animals

Written by Cathy Jones
Reading consultants: Christopher Collier and Alan Howe,
Bath Spa University, UK

First published by Parragon in 2010
Parragon
Queen Street House
4 Queen Street
Bath BA1 1HE, UK

ISBN 978-1-4075-9502-3

Printed in China

Jungle Animals

PaRragon

Bath New York Singapore Hong Kong Cologne Delhi Melbourne

Parents' notes

This book is part of a series of non-fiction books designed to appeal to children learning to read.

Each book has been developed with the help of educational experts.

At the end of each book is a quiz to help your child remember the information and the meanings of some of the words and sentences. There is also a glossary of difficult words relating to the subject matter in the book, and an index.

Contents

Life in the jungle

The jungle is a hot, steamy forest. It is also called the **rainforest**. Tall trees grow up to 80 metres above the forest floor. The rain takes 20 minutes to drip down to the ground.

The forest floor is dark as the tree branches block out the sun.

Amazing!

There are almost 10 million species of animal living in the rainforest, but only about 1.5 million have been named.

- Birds nest and bats roost in the tallest trees.

- Apes, monkeys and sloths climb in the canopy.

- Snakes, **frogs** and **insects** live in the branches and trunks.

- Wild cats, anteaters and other hunters prowl the forest floor.

- Crocodiles, turtles and fish swim in the swamps and rivers.

NORTH AMERICA

Atlantic Ocean

EUROPE

ASIA

TROPIC OF CANCER

Pacific Ocean

AFRICA

Pacific Ocean

EQUATOR

Indian Ocean

SOUTH AMERICA

TROPIC OF CAPRICORN

AUSTRALIA

Rainforests grow between the tropics and the equator, the hottest part of Earth.

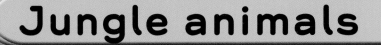

Jungle animals

All kinds of animals live in the jungle such as **mammals**, **reptiles**, birds and fish. Insects are the largest group of animals in the jungle.

Some animals have **adapted** so well to life in the jungle that they cannot live anywhere else.

Mammals, such as the golden lion tamarin, are covered in fur and feed their babies on milk.

The Indian gharial is a reptile. It hunts for fish in the river. It lays eggs on dry land.

Amazing!

Piranha fish are small, about 25 centimetres long. But they have rows of sharp teeth. A school of piranha can eat an animal as large as a sheep in minutes.

The harpy eagle is probably the largest flying rainforest bird. Its feathery wings measure up to 2 metres when they are spread out. It can carry away a monkey or sloth in its long talons.

Hunter and hunted

Life in the jungle can be hard. Animals that eat plants and insects are hunted by small meat-eating animals. These small animals are hunted by bigger **predators**.

The jaguar's spotted coat acts as **camouflage**. It eats animals such as the giant anteater.

The giant anteater has a long snout and sticky tongue – good for scooping up ants and termites.

Leafcutter ants can carry leaves 50 times heavier than themselves. They bury pieces of leaf and eat the **fungus** that grows on them. The ants then eat the fungus.

jaguar

Amazing!

The poison dart frog is a brightly coloured amphibian. Its colours warn enemies that it is poisonous to eat.

The Amazon

The largest rainforest in the world is in South America around the Amazon River. It is filled with lots of colourful life.

Capybaras belong to the same rodent family as mice and rats. They grow up to 60 centimetres tall.

Amazing!

Vampire bats feed on the blood of other animals.

The colourful, noisy toucan has a strong beak. It can easily open nutshells to eat the kernel inside.

The anaconda is the heaviest snake in the world. It can grow to 11 metres long. It squeezes its **prey** to death before eating it whole.

The rhinoceros beetle is the strongest animal in the world because it can carry 850 times its own weight. It grows up to 6 centimetres long.

Monkeys

Monkeys are **primates**, like us. They have hands like ours, with thumbs that bend away from their fingers. Their eyes are at the front of their heads. They live in family groups called troops.

These chimpanzees are grooming each other to keep clean and to relax.

The largest monkey in the world is the mandrill. It grows up to about 1 metre tall. The male mandrill has a colourful face and bottom, which gets brighter when it is excited.

The owl monkey is the only monkey that is active at night and sleeps in the day. Its big eyes help it to see in the dark.

The smallest monkey in the world is the pygmy marmoset. It is only 15 centimetres, not counting its 18-centimetre long tail.

The Congo

The Congo is the second largest rainforest in the world. Running through the rainforest is the second largest river in the world, the Congo River.

The gorilla is our closest relative in the animal world. They spend most of their time on the ground, walking on their knuckles for support.

Like its relative, the giraffe, the okapi has a very long tongue for pulling food from high trees and thorny bushes.

A chameleon changes the colour of its skin to blend into the surroundings if it feels threatened.

golden lion tamarin   Indian gharial   poison dart frog

harpy eagle   vampire bat   bandicoot   owl monkey

anaconda   rhinoceros beetle   piranha fish

giant anteater   leafcutter ants   clouded leopard

margay   okapi   chameleon   giant millepede

tree kangaroo   Bengal tiger   peacock   cassowary

orang-utan   water dragon   giant tree frog

ocelot   gorilla   toucan   mandrill

Amazing!

The African giant black millipede can grow to 39 centimetres and has two pairs of legs on each segment of its body.

Wild cats

Rainforest cats are hunters. They hunt alone at night. They have good night vision and mark the forest trails with their **scent** to warn off other animals.

Tigers are the largest cats in the world. The Bengal tiger can grow up to 3 metres long. It hunts for wild boar, oxen and monkeys.

Amazing!

The margay spends its whole life in the trees hunting birds and monkeys.

The clouded leopard is a good climber. It can run down a tree trunk headfirst.

The ocelot may look like a pet cat, but it is twice as big. It is also very fierce. It hunts small deer, rabbits and fish.

Indonesia

Indonesia is a ribbon of 17,000 islands in the Indian ocean. About one half of the land is covered in jungle. There are over 3,500 species of animal living here.

Orang-utans live in the rainforest trees. At night they make a nest to sleep in. They eat mainly fruit.

The deadly king cobra grows up to 5.6 metres long. Its two fangs can inject poison into its prey.

The peacock raises its magnificent tail feathers to attract a peahen to mate with.

Amazing!

The water dragon is 60 centimetres long. It can run away quickly on its back legs and hide underwater for up to 90 minutes.

Snakes

Rainforest snakes are good at hiding. They slither under fallen leaves, hide in hollow tree trunks and wind themselves around overhanging branches. They smell prey by flicking their tongue.

The cobra is a poisonous snake. When it is in danger, it makes itself look bigger by raising its head and puffing out its hood.

The deadly coral snake lives in the trees and on the forest floor. One bite from this viper snake is enough to kill an adult. It grows up to 91 cm long.

The green tree snake finds its food in the trees swallowing frogs and lizards head-first.

Australia

The Australian rainforest is home to many animals that are not seen in the rest of the world.

Amazing!

The cassowary is the largest land animal in Australia at 1.5 metres tall. It is a bird but it cannot fly.

Tree kangaroos are good climbers
and can jump from branch to branch.
The baby kangaroo, called a joey, is
carried in its mother's belly pouch.

The giant tree frog
is the biggest tree
frog in the world.
It grows up to 10
centimetres long.

Like a kangaroo, the
bandicoot carries its
babies in a pouch.
The bandicoot's
pouch is on its back
instead of its stomach.

Quiz

Now try this quiz!

All the answers can be found in this book

Which snake squeezes its prey to death?

(a) Anaconda
(b) Coral snake
(c) Green tree snake

Which monkey is the smallest?

(a) Chimpanzee
(b) Pygmy marmoset
(c) Owl monkey

Why does a chameleon change the colour of its skin?

(a) For fun
(b) When it feels threatened
(c) To attract a mate

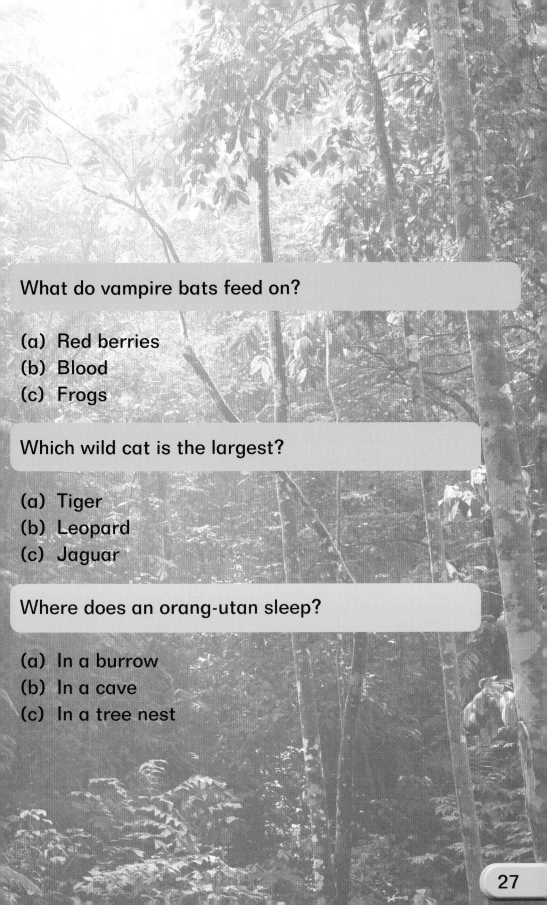

What do vampire bats feed on?

(a) Red berries
(b) Blood
(c) Frogs

Which wild cat is the largest?

(a) Tiger
(b) Leopard
(c) Jaguar

Where does an orang-utan sleep?

(a) In a burrow
(b) In a cave
(c) In a tree nest

Glossary

Adapted Changed in a way that helps the animal to survive where it lives.

Amphibian A group of animals (e.g. frogs) that lay eggs in water and can live on land.

Camouflage An animal's pattern or colour that helps it to hide against the background.

Fungus A living thing a bit like a plant. Fungi are not green. Mushrooms and toadstools are fungi.

Insect A group of small animals with six legs. Many insects have wings.

Mammal A group of animals that have a back bone, give birth to babies and feed them on milk.

Predator   An animal that hunts another
animal for food.

Prey   An animal that is hunted by
another animal for food.

Primate   A group of animals that includes
humans, monkeys and apes.

Rainforest   An area of evergreen forest near
the tropics where there is a
lot of rainfall.

Reptile   A group of animals covered in
scales that includes lizards, snakes
and crocodiles.

Scent   The smell that an animal leaves to
tell other animals it has been in
a place.

Index

Acknowledgements

t=top, c=centre, b=bottom, r=right, l=left

Front cover: Getty Images/Andy Rouse
Back cover: l Getty Images/Laura Wickenden, r Getty Images/
Cyril Laubscher

1 istockphoto/ Kenneth O'Quinn, 2 Getty Images/ William Weber,
3 istockphoto/ Erik van Hannen, 4 istockphoto/Tokle, 5 tl istockphoto/
Erik van Hannen, 5 cl Getty Images/ Frans Lemmens, 5 br Getty
Images/Joel Sartore, 6-7 istockphoto/ SZE FEI WONG,
6bl istockphoto/ Kenneth O'Quinn, 7 tr istockphoto/ Finn Brandt,
8-9 istockphoto/ Ray Roper, 8 b istockphoto/ Erik van Hannen,
9 cl Getty Images/Joel Sartore, 9 cr istockphoto/Simon Podgorsek,
10-11 Getty Images/Tim Laman, 10 cl istockphoto/Sondra Paulson,
10 b Getty Images/Peter Lilja, 11 br istockphoto/Steve Geer,
12-13 Getty Images/M G Therin Weise, 12 br istockphoto/Michael
Lynch, 13 tr istockphoto/Roberto A Sanchez, 13 cl Getty Images/Gary
Braasch, 13 br istockphoto/Tokle, 14-15 Getty Images/VEER John
Giustina, 14 cl istockphoto/Catharina van den Dikkenberg,
15 tr Getty Images/Art Wolfe, 15 cr istockphoto/Michael Lynch,
16-17 istockphoto/Guenter Guni, 16 cl istockphoto/Gary Martin,
16bl istockphoto/Kenneth O'Quinn, 17 br AFP/Getty Images,
18-19 Getty Images/Jami Tarris, 18 br Getty Images/Carol Farneti-
Foster, 19 tr istockphoto/dieter Spears, 19cr Getty Images/Tom
Brakefield, 20-21istockphoto/George Clerk, 20 br Getty Images/Tom
Brakefield, 21 br Getty Images/Frans Lemmens, 22 Getty Images/
Bnsdeo, 23 cl Getty Images/William Weber, 23 tr Getty Images/
Jim Merli, 23 b Getty Images/Joel Sartore, 24-25 istockphoto/
Susan Flashman, 24 bl Getty Images/Jason Edwards, 25tr National
Geographic/Getty Images